A BluePrir  to SELLING ON AMAZON

A Basic Guide to Selling on Amazon and Side Income Part Time

By

George Pain

BOOK DESCRIPTION

Amazon, the world's largest online marketplace, has achieved its prominence and success thanks to dedicated sellers across the globe. They have made it a market of choice, thus providing products that meet buyers' needs. With over 300 billion sales in 2016 and projected to grow in double digits for the foreseeable future, this is a place where anyone who would like to make passive income ought to be.

To ensure that you get the best out of becoming an Amazon Seller, this book, "A BluePrint to Selling on Amazon" provides all the information you need to not only start selling on Amazon but also to successfully build a business that enables you to make at least $2000 a month profit on side income, part time.

This guide recognizes that there are millions out there who have heard of great successes made by many sellers on Amazon but don't know how it can benefit them in their own unique ways. Thus, it starts off from the basics by outlining to you the benefits of selling on Amazon that have made it become the number one choice for online sellers.

While many would-be sellers are inspired by stories of the many benefits that accrue to Amazon sellers, the question that most ask is "where do I find products to sell on Amazon?" This is an extremely important question as you cannot sell what you don't have. Luckily, unlike traditional brick-and-mortar storefronts, doing business online on platforms such as on Amazon brings products you are searching for within your reach. You can easily find products to sell right at the click of your button. The guide provides you with places where you get everything you need to sell on Amazon.

There is no market that sells everything. That's hardly possible. Amazon is no exception. In this regard, you need to know the categories of items you cannot sell and those that you can only sell under certain terms. To save you the agony of bringing to Amazon a product that you cannot sell, Amazon provides information about restricted categories. That is, categories of items with certain restrictions which must be abided by for you to be able to sell.

Technology continues to shape the way we conduct business. Amazon's way of doing business is based on technology. To enable you have a great seller experience, Amazon has created Amazon Seller App that can enable you to fully transact on Amazon – sell, monitor customer orders, monitor shipping progress, check on your disbursement schedule, and monitor your cash-flow – all while on the go. You simply need to download Amazon Seller App right from your mobile Apps store. This guide shows you how to use Amazon Seller App to boost your sales.

Monitoring your product performance is the key to making informed decisions. Business is about making informed decisions promptly and as accurate as possible. Amazon has Sales Rank, a tool that enables you to see how your product is performing relative to other products in your niche. Information provided in this book enables you to properly interpret your Amazon Sales Rank and use it to make appropriate decisions that can meet consumer demands, scale up your business, boost sales and make earning $2000 per month passive income a walk in the park.

Pricing your product is so far the greatest of all decisions you can make in your entire selling process. Without pricing, you are not a seller. Pricing determines how much your entire selling process rewards you. It determines your profitability. This guide shows you how to price your product so that you can be able you to make $2000 a month profit on side income, part time, in a manner that takes advantage of all opportunities available to you.

Enjoy your reading!

GIFT INCLUDED

If you are an entrepreneur, an aspiring entrepreneur, someone who is trying to create additional income stream or even someone who just loves self improvement books; then you need to read my recommendations for top 10 business books ever. These are book that I have read that have changed my life for the better.

Top 10 Business Books

ABOUT THE AUTHOR

George Pain is an entrepreneur, author and business consultant. He specializes in setting up online businesses from scratch, investment income strategies and global mobility solutions. He has built several businesses from the ground up, and is excited to share his knowledge with readers. Here is a list of his books.

Books of George Pain

DISCLAIMER

Contents

INTRODUCTION

It is no doubt that the days of permanent stable jobs are slowly winding down to an end. While the employer wants productivity, the employee wants higher incomes, independence and flexibility. Whoever can merge the four – productivity, higher incomes, independence and flexibility becomes the modern-day king of the market. Everyone is in a market, be it of products (merchants) or services (employees and professional consultants). To earn higher incomes, you need to boost your income opportunities and your earning potential. Online income opportunities have become the best way to maximize your income, part-time. Amazon leads the pack in providing you these opportunities through marketing and selling of consumer products.

You need a Blueprint to Selling on Amazon to be able to be not just a seller earning passive income on Amazon but a shrewd seller optimizing the best of available opportunities. This guide empowers you with hands-on practical information on how you can start selling on Amazon and make $2000 a month profit on side income, part time.

Your road to financial freedom begins with your determination to be free. Information is the power that you need to set yourself free. This book is a blueprint to that success.

Keep reading!

WHY SHOULD I SELL ON AMAZON?

With over 1.5 million products listed, Amazon is a marketplace of choice for thousands of sellers. A marketplace can't attract such a huge number of sellers without great benefits to them.

The benefits of selling on Amazon are many. The following are just but a few;

- Large global market
- Robust logistics infrastructure
- Ease of automation
- Plenty of earning opportunities
- Cut down on fixed (overhead) costs
- Secure and timely payments
- Stress-free shipping
- Great performance reports
- Good partnership support
- Opportunities for multiple passive income streams

Large global market

Amazon is a global online market in consumer goods with over 1.5 million unique visitors a day. Selling your products on Amazon means you are simply presenting your products to the availability of these customers wherever they happen to be across the globe.

Robust logistics infrastructure

To deliver products on the international market requires an elaborate logistics system. Managing logistics is one of the greatest challenges of international trade. Cost, time delays, unreliable partners are some of the common challenges. Amazon has a reliable logistics infrastructure that is already configured to deliver the kind of products availed on its market.

Ease of automation

When you are starting off as a small-scale seller, the biggest challenge is being able to carry out myriad of tasks required of international trade all on your own. This becomes almost impossible without the aid of technology. Amazon has sophisticated technology that enables automation of common tasks such as monitoring orders, sales and responses. Amazon API has also enabled third party automation tools to be developed that can help you automate virtually any task that you carry out on Amazon, ranging from niche search, product search, listing, pricing, feedback, etc. Furthermore, specialists and consultants who can be able to do all the work on your behalf do exist.

Amazon has created an Amazon Seller App that enables sellers to easily list and monitor their products. Apart from this App, Amazon has opened up its Amazon Web Service API, which enables third parties to create automation tools (apps) that enable a seller to automate virtually any kind of selling activity on Amazon. This makes one to make more money at less sweat.

Plenty of earning opportunities

Currently, Amazon has 1.5 million listed items with about 2 billion items sold per month. There is growth rate of over 10% per annum. This means that the customer base continues to grow, thus, more growth in demand. More and more people are getting accustomed to online marketplaces as the world continues to become digitized and new shopping opportunities continue to be presented via ecommerce. As more people join ecommerce, physical logistics networks continue to become dense. This is due to increased viability as a result of economies of scale. This means that, on-door deliveries become a reality to many. When people get confident that they can receive their orders within a very short time right where they are, their trust in ecommerce as opposed to brick-and-mortar shops grows. This creates increased demand and newer opportunities for sellers to exploit. Amazon Prime has revolutionized this. As Amazon Prime continues to cover more territories, so do more customers join in thus expanding the reach of physical delivery via ecommerce.

Clampdown on fixed overhead costs

The Amazon model of charging sellers who use its platform is variable in nature with a very small fixed component. What worries most businesses are the fixed overhead costs. These are costs which must be incurred whether one makes sales or not. Such overhead costs include warehousing costs, labor costs in terms of salaries associated with logistics management, and such others. Amazon charges the bulk of these costs based on successful sales. This means that if there is no sale, then majority of the fixed overhead costs are not incurred. Variable costs are only incurred based on transaction and volumes.

Secure and timely payments

Every businessperson is always worried about receivables. Claiming payment is never such an easy task, especially when it comes to dealing with international trade. Amazon has an elaborate system which ensures that you get paid without the attendant cost of managing bad and doubtful debts.

Stress-free shipping

The biggest factor that discourages most sellers from engaging in international trade is the complexity of shipping. Amazon handles this complexity on your behalf.

Great performance reports

Like any businessperson, you would like to get up-to-date information about your business performance, more so, your sales. Amazon has elaborate, robust and sophisticated reporting tools that can help you gain deep insight about performance of your product. This helps you to make informed decision about the kind of products to add to your inventory and the kind of products to retire from your inventory.

Good partnership support

Amazon has partnered with many different service providers. These include; shipping companies, payment processors, and third-party tools providers, among others. This means that you have a better chance to get help that you need in regard to shipping, payments and automation.

Opportunities for multiple passive income streams

Every seller is an investor in one form or another. As a seller, you not only invest your money, but also time and effort. Like any other investor, you would like to minimize risks of less or no income on your investment. Diversification becomes the natural choice to mitigate this risk. Through automation, Amazon provides one with an opportunity to earn multiple passive income streams without more time and effort. Indeed, the fastest way to reach and be guaranteed of making $2000 a month profit on side income part time is opening up multiple income streams through automation.

The more products you list in different categories and the more you are able to source for these products from different suppliers, the more likely you are able to gain greater profit margins.

HOW MANY PRODUCTS SHOULD I SELL?

Amazon is a huge global marketplace with more than 1.5 million products listed for sale. It also has over 150 million unique visitors per month with over 300 million customer accounts. This means that opportunities to list your products are immense. However, the number of products to list depends on the following factors;

- Your Amazon seller plan
- Your product niche
- Your budget
- The Amazon Marketplace
- The delivery logistics
- Your degree of automation
- Your marketing effort

Your Amazon Seller Plan

Not all sellers are equal. Some are large-scale while others are small-scale sellers. Thus, Amazon has established plans to suit sellers based on their scale of operations.

Your seller plan greatly determines the number of items that you can list for sale. There are two main Amazon seller plans;

- **Individual** – this is for you, if you plan to sell fewer than 40 items per month

- **Professional** – this is for you if you plan to sell more than 40 items per month

The individual plan limits you to a maximum of 20 categories of items to sell. The professional plan has 10 extra categories in addition to the individual plan.

The ability to list many products at a go doesn't exist on individual plan. However, with professional plan there are bulk tools that can enable you to list many items at a go.

Furthermore, the number of products that you should sell can be limited by reporting. You obviously want to monitor performance of existing products before adding more or determining whether your business is worth or not. Professional plan has many reporting tools provided by Amazon by default. These tools are not available to individual plans.

Unlike professional plan, individual plan is not pegged to Amazon Prime by default. Amazon statistics indicates that almost 60% of its revenue is generated from Amazon Prime customers. Without easy access to your products by Amazon Prime customers, then, you are disadvantaged in accessing almost 60% of Amazon's potential customer base. This limits the number of products that you can sell on Amazon, at least in terms of volume (as sales volume depends on demand).

The rule of thumb for your choice of seller plan;

If you anticipate selling less than 40 items per month, go for individual plan. However, if you anticipate selling more than 40 items per month, go for professional plan. If you are a starter, it is prudent to start with individual plan and then scale up to professional plan when you are certain that your sales per month are consistently above 40 items and likely to grow.

Your product niche

If you intend to sell products already on Amazon, then, the number of possible items to sell will be limited to the number of products available within your product niche (category). However, in case you intent sell products not available on Amazon, this will not be limited by the number of items within your product niche for so long as your niche doesn't fall within restricted category.

Your budget

Your very own budget determines how many products that you can sell on Amazon. You can only stretch as much as your budget allows. Thus, priced the same, the higher the budget the more the items you can sell on Amazon and vice versa.

The Amazon Marketplace

Amazon marketplace, like any other market, is determined by the forces of supply and demand. The supply depends on demand.

Thus, the number of products that you can sell on Amazon also depends on the consumer demand. Being able to get information on how many products an average seller sales within a given category can be a good yardstick for this. The quickest way to tell this is to divide the number of items sold within your niche by the number of sellers within the same niche over a given period of time (e.g. 3 months). In addition to Amazon statistical reports (which may not be such specific), there are many Amazon third-party tools that help you achieve this.

The delivery logistics

The number of products that you can sell depends on how fast and how much you can deliver to your customers. These logistics depends on distance, quantity, cost, mode of transport and the nature of items. The longer the distance, the more time it takes to deliver and the fewer the delivery cycles. Some items only make economic sense when delivered in a certain quantity (Economic Order Quantity). As such, if the demand takes time to reach the Economic Order Quantity (EOC), you will have to sell less.

Given the same quantity and mode of transport, some items cost more than others. Thus, you will be more inclined to deliver less of them depending on your working capital. Delivery by sea accommodates higher volumes per delivery as compared to delivery by air. This means that you can easily deliver more quantities to a large market by sea compared to by air, especially if you are dealing with bulky, low value products. On the other hand, delivery by air allows you to carry out many delivery cycles, this is ideal for high value, low weight items. Items that are flammable (such as petroleum products and flammable chemicals) are not accepted on planes. They can only be transported in special tankers, on road or over sea. This can limit how much of such items you can deliver to the market in a given time due to time lag occasioned by sea and road transport.

Your degree of automation

Automation has been successfully used to achieve higher levels of mass production. This too is being used to achieve higher levels of sales. No one understands the importance of automating sales process than Amazon. Amazon has employed 4500 robots in its warehouses just to handle delivery. Amazon too has created Amazon Seller App to increase automation on the seller side. It has opened up its Amazon API (Application Programming Interface) to allow third-party apps developers to create automation apps and link them up to its platform. The best way to make $2000 a month profit on side income as fast as possible is to emulate Amazon's way of doing business – automation.

If you happen to be a solopreneur (doing all seller activities alone), then, you are so constrained by human limitations such as tiredness, errors, working hours, sickness, monotony, boredom, etc. However, when you choose to automate your process, both mechanically and human-wise, you end up overcoming these limitations and thus enjoy higher levels of sales, multiple income streams and greater success as an entrepreneur. There are many processes that you can automate. These include niche search, product selection, private labeling, Inventory management,

Consumer insight (consumer metrics), Marketing, Copywriting and keyword management, Customer interaction, International payment processing, among others.

Examples of automation tools that you can use to make your business a great success include niche search tools such as Niche Hunter, Niche Wolf, Amasuite; product selection tools such as Jungle Scout Web App, Jungle Scout Chrome extension, CamelCamelCamel; listing tools such as Ecomdash, Sellbrite, Scanlister, Listtee; SEO (Search Engine Optimization) keyword management tools such as AMZ Tracker, MerchantWords, Sonar, Scientific Seller, SeoChart, Rank Tracker, Google Keyword Planner; pricing tools such as Jungle Scout, RepricerExpress, Stitchlabs, MarketHustl; inventory management tools such as Restock, Teikametrics, Ecomdash, Veeqo, Finale Inventory, Forecastly; consumer insight tools such as Amazooka, AMZtracker; marketing/advertisement tools such as Amazon Advertising, Unicorn Smasher; and consumer interaction tools such as FeedbackGenius, Salesbacker, Tomoson.

Amazon would not have become a multibillion dollar global enterprise without significant level of automation. You too can achieve great success following on the footsteps of Amazon and relying on its framework through automation.

Your promotional effort

With millions of products on Amazon, you cannot optimize your sales without promotion. Promotion is one of the core components of effective marketing. Discounts, free samples, bundling, gifts, referrals, advertisements, niche website, among other promotional efforts are key to standing out of the crowd. You must gain competitive advantage for you to be able to sell more and list more. You not only have to depend on existing demand, you also have to induce demand by creating curiosity, interest and desires in the mind of the potential buyer via sales promotion. Luckily, you too can automate this promotional effort by using automation tools and outsourcing the promotion effort.

WHERE DO I FIND PRODUCTS TO SELL ON AMAZON?

To be able to know where to find products to sell on Amazon, you must first be able to know what products that you want to sell. Once you get to know what products to sell on Amazon, then, based on Amazon system, you can find out how to bring those products on Amazon. The means of bringing products on Amazon will greatly shape where to find them.

What should I sell on Amazon?

To determine what to sell on Amazon is the first and foremost step every seller undertakes. You can't even open a Seller's account if you don't have a rough idea of what you should sell.

To be able to know what to sell on Amazon, you have to do niche research. After carrying out niche research, you select your niche based on your research findings.

The following criteria will help you establish your niche;

- Passion – there are certain items that you are passionate about. You would just wish to convince every person to have them. You enjoy them. You benefit greatly from them. You feel that people can be better off having them. These are the items that will help you find your niche. Put them on your list for further research on their performance and profitability.

- Skills and talents – do you have a skill or talent that you can use to create a product? If you do, research on such kind of product for its performance and profitability. If such product doesn't exist on the market, then, you have a big chance to introduce it into the market. Experiment now. It could be your breakthrough. The advantage of novel products is that you have control over their pricing for there is no competition. You can patent it to avoid unwarranted replications, price undercuts and unnecessary competition.

- Experience – having experience in dealing with a certain product, either as a consumer, employee or manufacturer provides you with vantage information about its features, consumer responses, and cost, among others. Check out on how such similar products perform on Amazon marketplace and establish its performance and profitability.

- Funds – what range of item prices can you afford in reasonable stock? Can you afford the overall Economic Order Quantity (EOQ) of the items? Answering these questions can enable you determine whether certain items meet their working capital needs (stocking and shipping) or not. Each kind of item has its own EOQ depending on its size, volume of consumption, mode of transportation, etc.

- Potential market – do you have a potential market in mind? If it were not for Amazon, do you think you could be able to sell same items in other markets? Remember, Amazon is an online Storefront. While there could be "walk-in" customers (that is, customers who are already on Amazon Marketplace and ready to visit your listing), you also need to make effort in soliciting for, inviting and directing customers to your storefront. If you are active on Social Media and you have many fans, or, you are active in other offline social activities; can the fans, members, friends, frequent visitors, among others, be able to buy something from you? What is that something that you think that most of them would be so happy to buy? This is already a potential market that you need to find an appropriate niche to serve.

A single product that you know can help you establish a niche (range of products with similar attributes). On the other hand, knowledge of a niche can help you establish products to fit into that niche. So, either way, you can be able to find items to sell on Amazon.

Once you are able to establish your product niche, then, you can refine it further to list down the kind of products that you can sell within that niche.

How do I get items to sell on Amazon?

After answering the "what", the next question to address is 'how do I get products to sell on Amazon". Yes, after "what" naturally comes "how". Depending on how you can get the product, you can now easily find out where you can find them.

The following are ways by which you can get products outside Amazon marketplace and sell them on Amazon.

- Suppliers/manufacturers
- Private Labeling
- Contract manufacturing
- Retail Arbitrage

Suppliers/manufacturers

There are certain products whose suppliers/ manufacturers haven't listed them on Amazon. This is more so for items not manufactured or supplied within the geographical location of the respective Amazon marketplace. For example, if you are dealing with Amazon.com marketplace (US), there is a fair chance that some manufacturers/suppliers outside US have not listed their products for direct supply on Amazon.com. You can take advantage of this by buying from them and then selling on Amazon.com, that is, if you are able to make good profit margin.

Private Labeling

Private labeling happens when you get goods directly from manufacturers, rebrand them under your own private label and sell them on Amazon as your own. Good examples of such is buying plain T-shirts, Blank unprinted DVDs, plain cover exercise books and then printing on them your brand details.

Contract Manufacturing

Contract manufacturing is close to Private Label, except that you enter into a formal contract with a manufacturer of a certain product so that products are manufactured on your behalf under certain specification. Branding is done on your behalf (and as per your specifications) by the manufacturer. Thus, the goods are manufactured by you but under contract (use of someone else's manufacturing factory).

Retail Arbitrage

Retail arbitrage refers to taking an order from a customer in a marketplace (e.g. Amazon) where a certain product is relatively more expensive and ordering for the same product in another marketplace (e.g. EBay) where the product is relatively cheaper to be delivered to your customer.

Retail Arbitrage, though not illegal, is informal. This exposes the trader to higher risks in case the price in the cheaper marketplace suddenly shoots up before an order is made. Nonetheless, there are those shrewd entrepreneurs who continue to make millions of dollars from Amazon retail arbitrage.

Where to find items to sell on Amazon

Now that you have answer the 'What' and the 'How' of the product, the next logical step is to answer the 'Where' of the product.

The following are major marketplaces where you can find potential suppliers.

- Alibaba – Alibaba is the world's largest source of suppliers. It has centers in many parts of the world, including US, Mexico, Canada and Europe. Thus, it is easy to order products on Alibaba just as a local would do and deliver them to Amazon. Most of the time, it will be up to the supplier who has listed the product in a given marketplace to deliver to it.

- Global sources – Global resource is another huge source of suppliers. It is not as huge as Alibaba, but, it is a great alternative if you are unable to source for items from Alibaba.

- Aliexpress – Aliexpress is a subsidiary of Alibaba. It extends its presence in those localities which Alibaba can't effectively serve (probably, due to jurisdictional issues).

- Made-In-China – Made-In-China is a marketplace focused on availing platform for Chinese or China-based suppliers to provide their products to the rest of the world. It too has offices across North America (Canada) and Europe, among other localities.

- HKTDC – This is another marketplace based in Hong-Kong, China. Like Made-In-China, it is a platform for Chinese or China-based suppliers (more so, from Hong Kong) to avail their products to the rest of the world.

- EBay (for retail arbitrage) – EBay is Amazon's greatest competitor. If you want to take benefit of price differential between the two markets for quick profits, then, EBay is obviously your best choice to find products.

How to choose a supplier for your product

Once you have determined where to get your products, the next step is to choose the right supplier for your product.

Criteria for choosing your supplier

You have to setup criteria for choosing the right supplier well in advance to avoid being carried away by impulses. The following criteria will help you get the most deserved supplier;

- Niche fitness – the best supplier is a one who perfectly fits your niche, that is, other considerations aside, you can fully order all your niche products from that particular supplier.

- Reliability – it is important that your potential supplier is reliable. In this case, the supplier must be capable of being a 'going concern', that is, the supplier should be capable of existing in the long-run. You have to determine how long the supplier has existed in the market, how capable the supplier is in terms of meeting your order. You can determine this by checking supplier's financial reports over time, supplier's history of supply volumes, among others.

- Price stability – you need to determine the supplier behavior in terms price stability. Is the potential supplier stable price-wise? Has the supplier's price been relatively stable over time? This will help you avoid the trappings of temporary offers.

- Service reputation – Has the supplier been able to satisfactorily meet supply obligations? Customer reviews, supplier ranking, etc, are some of the things that can help you determine the supplier's service reputation.

- Supply Order capability – A supplier can meet all the previously mentioned criteria, yet fail in terms of your volume requirements. Check the volume of successful orders to determine whether the supplier is capable of fulfilling your volume of order. Minimum Order Quantity (MOQ) stipulated by the supplier can also help you determine the supplier capacity. A supplier that has higher MOQ than your EOQ (Economic Order Quantity) is a supplier high above your Order category. On the other hand, if the supplier has a MXOQ (Maximum Order Quantity) level that is lower than your MOQ, that simply means the supplier is way below your Order category. The most capable suppliers are those whom their MOQ and your MOQ are close but yours is slightly above and their MXOQ is higher than your EOQ.

- Affordability – Once you narrowed down to a few suppliers based on the above criteria, you have to consider affordability based on the cost (price plus shipping and insurance). This cost should be based on your EOQ. The supplier with the lowest cost based on your EOQ should have preference.

- Quality – You need to ascertain that you are getting the right value for your money. If possible, request a sample from each of the suppliers you have shortlisted based on the above criteria. Some suppliers may lower the quality of an item for it to appear cheaper than the rest. If you can afford, it is more prudent to buy random products from your shortlisted suppliers to test them out than to order for sample. This is because the supplier is more likely to customize a sample just to suit your requirements. Such a sample may not represent the products that are normally supplied and which you are likely going to order later on.

- Ordering terms – You need to confirm that the supplier's Ordering terms meet your needs. These ordering terms include Minimum Order Quantity, Batch quantity, Order processing time, etc.

- Delivery terms – Delivery terms are important if you have to meet your customer needs. You need to confirm shipping and delivery terms from your potential supplier. These include the delivery lead, place of delivery, Returns policy, etc.

- Payment terms - Payment terms are important in helping you determine your cash-flow and evaluate your cash risk (risk that you cash payment may not get commensurate value in return). Payment terms include factors such as down payment, escrow payment, payment in advance, refunds, mode of payment (bank, PayPal, etc).

- Proximity to Amazon collection points – In most cases, Amazon has specific places from which it can pick up your inventory. Furthermore, these pick-up points are not available in every country. Thus, the more proximate your supplier is to an Amazon pick-up point the more likely you are going to incur less shipping cost.

The steps taken in choosing the right supplier

The following steps will help you choose the right supplier and make an Order;

1. Prepare a list of niche products that you want to be supplied.

2. Access the marketplace where you can find suppliers for your listed items (see "Where to find items to sell on Amazon").

3. Search for each item on your list to get its suppliers

4. List suppliers for each product (not more than 10, if there are more than 10 potential suppliers, make a quick sieve to get just 10 of them)

5. Review the list of suppliers of each product based on your supplier selection criteria so that you can make a shortlist of about three whom you will contact to get further details

6. Contact potential suppliers on your shortlist to introduce yourself, provide product details and make enquiries about price details, Order terms, delivery terms and payment terms, among others.

7. Request for product samples (if possible) – most suppliers are willing to provide samples. If you have the potential to order large quantities in future, they won't resist providing you with free samples. Yet, it is still prudent, if you can, to make your own random purchases in the market to test the quality. This is so because no supplier would likely give you a standard sample. They would like to present the best of their products which, in certain cases, may mislead you in terms of the standard product quality.

8. Choose your supplier from your shortlist of potential suppliers

9. Negotiate the price – offered price is usually based on certain terms, e.g. Order quantity, delivery and payment terms. See if you can negotiate the price based on these terms.

10. Order the product – once in agreement on Order terms, delivery terms, payment terms and price, the next logical step is to place an Order.

WHAT ARE RESTRICTED CATEGORIES?

To manage a huge marketplace such as Amazon is not easy. Thus, certain rules have to be made to ensure orderliness, effective utility of the platform and its resources, fair competition and value for both buyers and sellers. Thus, Amazon has come up with restricted categories to ensure that all these needs are met.

Restricted categories are those categories where certain conditions must be met before one can be allowed to list in them.

These restricted categories are categories;

1. Which you only have access depending on your seller plan, or;
2. Where you need approval in order to list, or;
3. Where you can only list products of certain condition (e.g. new, used, refurbished, collectible), or;
4. Where new sellers are not being accepted (until further notice)

Categories in which you have access to depending on your seller plan

- Both Individual and professional sellers have unlimited access to 20 categories

- Professional sellers have access to 10 more categories which individual sellers are restricted

Categories available to both individual and professional sellers

1. Amazon Device accessories
2. Amazon Kindle -used only
3. Baby products - new only
4. Books - new, used
5. Camera and photo - new, used, refurbished
6. Cell-phones - new, used, refurbished, unlocked
7. Electronics (accessories) – new, used, refurbished
8. Electronics (consumer) – new, used, refurbished
9. Handmade and Hand-altered products – new only
10. Health and personal care – new only
11. Home and Garden – new, used, refurbished, collectible
12. Industrial and scientific – new only
13. Musical instruments –new, used, refurbished, collectible
14. Office products – new, used, refurbished, collectible
15. Outdoors (action sports, cycling, outdoor gear, outdoor apparel) – new, used, refurbished
16. Personal computers (desktops, laptops, tablets) – new, used, refurbished
17. Professional services – professionals only

18. Tools and home improvements (building materials, appliance parts, electrical, plumbing, hand and power tools) – new, used, refurbished
19. Toys and games
20. Video games and video game consoles – new, used, collectible

Categories available to professional sellers only

There are certain categories that only professional sellers have access to. This simply means that they are out of bound for individual sellers.

1. Automotive and powersports – new, used, refurbished, collectible, approval required
2. Beauty - new only, approval required
3. Clothing & accessories - new only, approval required
4. Business-to-business products - new, used, refurbished
5. Grocery & Gourmet food - new only, approval required
6. Jewelry – new only, approval required
7. Luggage and Travel accessories – new only, approval required
8. Shoes, handbags, sunglasses – new only, approval required

9. Video, DVD, and Blu-Ray – new, used, collectible, approval required

10. Watches – new only, approval required

11. Wine – new, collectible, approval required

Categories that you need approval before listing

All categories available to professional sellers only require approval.

Categories where you can list only new items

The following are categories where you can list only new items;

1. Baby products - new only

2. Handmade and Hand-altered products – new only

3. Health and personal care – new only

4. Industrial and scientific – new only

5. Beauty - new only, approval required

6. Clothing & accessories - new only, approval required

7. Jewelry – new only, approval required

8. Luggage and Travel accessories – new only, approval required

9. Shoes, handbags, sunglasses – new only, approval required

10. Watches – new only, approval required

Categories where you can only list used items

1. Amazon Kindle

Categories where new sellers are not accepted (until further notice)

1. Collectible coins
2. Fine art
3. Historical and advertising collectibles
4. Music – new, used, collectible
5. Sports collectibles

It is extremely important to check restricted category before laboring to find items for sale. This is more so if you are listing products not already on Amazon. This will greatly reduce the stresses and strains of bringing products to Amazon only for them to be rejected after spending so much on buying and shipping.

USING AMAZON SELLER APP

Amazon Seller App is a mobile App developed by Amazon. This App has revolutionized the way sellers interact with their Amazon accounts. With Amazon Seller App you are on the move with your business. You are not only able to respond quickly to your customers as you would do with an easy reach of SMS, you can do a host of many other things with your Amazon Seller App.

The following are what Amazon Seller App empowers you to do on the go;

- Secure access to your Amazon Seller account
- Search for new items to sell on Amazon
- List items for sale
- Estimate your item profitability
- Manage orders
- Manage inventory
- Quick cash-flow management
- Easily tell items that are ineligible
- Respond to customers
- Seek help from Amazon

Secure access to your Amazon Seller account

In this era of intense phishing and hacking, online security is of utmost importance. Amazon seller app, unlike other apps, routes all your activities through high-security Amazon servers. This helps to safeguard your account from phishing and hacking. Phishing and Hacking can steal your information and habits on Amazon to be sold to competitors for purposes of disadvantaging or damaging your business.

Search for new items to sell on Amazon

Amazon Seller App enables you to quickly search for items by typing in text or simply scanning the item's barcode. This way, you can quickly get the product information including Sales Rank, current price, and customer reviews, among other critical information that can help you make an informed decision.

Listing of your items for sale

With Amazon Seller App, you don't need to go to the browser to list your items. You can simply list your items while on the go. You too can easily scan barcodes of the items you want to list and their details (if they are already on Amazon) get quickly listed on your behalf. You can then customize to your preference.

Estimate your profitability

The most important information that you need before listing your product for sale on Amazon is its profitability. Amazon Seller App enables you to quickly estimate profitability of a given item before deciding to launch it for sale. This saves you from the risks of inadvertently selling at a loss.

Manage orders

The greatest way to boost customer experience and satisfaction and eventually get rewarded via positive reviews is to ensure that delivery is made on time. Also, in case of unfortunate delays, you are able to communicate well in advance to the customers. Amazon Seller App has facility that can enable you easily view pending orders, confirm shipment and receive notification when the sale closes. This way, you are able to remain above board in as far as communicating effectively with your customers which is the core essence of successful customer service.

Respond to customers

Customers have a right to be notified in the most timely and effective manner. Amazon Seller App enables you to respond quickly to customers queries. This quickens their buy decisions and also helps to mitigate on likely negative feedbacks should anything go wrong or something happens that has the potential to lower customer experience.

Manage inventory

Managing your inventory is not only core to your profit maximization but also to protection of your investment. Amazon App allows you reorganize your inventory items (sort and filter) and optimize prices and quantities on the go. This enables you to enjoy the benefits of changes in consumer demand while securing your investment.

Quick cash-flow management

In business, it is quite punitive when you fail to disburse cash, especially for supplies, when due. This can mean your contract being suspended, being surcharged, or your order being delayed or cancelled. This can obviously have adverse effect on your inventory and possibly negative customer experience. Amazon Seller App enables you to quickly view your potential disbursements so that you can make appropriate cash-flow decisions.

Easily tell items that are ineligible

Amazon Seller App is strategically designed to enable you to quickly know about items that are off limit to you depending on your seller plan. This becomes extremely handy when it comes to searching and deciding on items to list.

Seek help from Amazon

Getting help when you need it is the greatest benefit one can derive from a service provider. Amazon, via its platform, has presented you, through Amazon Seller App, an opportunity to easily seek and access help while on the go.

HOW TO USE AMAZON SALES RANK

The performance of a product within a given category is ranked by Amazon so as to enable sellers to easily evaluate it. This ranking is what is referred to Amazon Sales Rank, more commonly known as Amazon Best Sellers Rank.

How to interpret Amazon Sales Rank

The lower the rank, the higher is the performance of a given product relative to other products within the same category. On the other hand, the higher the rank, the lower is the performance of a given product relative to others within the same category. A category's bestseller rank is 1 (the lowest).

Fig. 6.1 depicts a typical products details profile on Amazon. You can see that the Amazon Best Sellers Rank as #1,427,263. This is obviously an extremely high rank indicating that the product is performing poorly compared to other products with the same category (kindle eBooks).

Product details

File Size: 5044 KB
Print Length: 69 pages
Publisher: Betafortunes Publications (July 19, 2016)
Publication Date: July 19, 2016
Sold by: Amazon Digital Services LLC
Language: English
ASIN: B01IRIQWJ4
Text-to-Speech: Enabled
X-Ray: Not Enabled
Word Wise: Enabled
Lending: Not Enabled
Enhanced Typesetting: Not Enabled
Amazon Best Sellers Rank: #1,427,263 Paid in Kindle Store (See Top 100 Paid in Kindle Store)

As a rule of thumb, any product ranking higher than one million is performing poorly within that category. Though, this depends on the number of items listed within that category as some categories have more items than others.

Important facts you need to know about Amazon Sales Rank

It is important to know how Amazon Sales Rank comes about so that you can be able to better understand your product's Sales Rank;

- Sales Rank is dynamic
- Sales Rank is relative
- Sales Rank is frequency-sensitive
- Sales Rank is stability-dependent
- Sales Rank is sensitive to customer experience

Sales Rank is dynamic

Amazon Sales Rank changes over time. It is not static. Amazon adjusts this rank every hour with a time lag of 1 to 3 hours. When a sale of a product is made, the rank goes lower. However, when another product within the same category is sold, this is likely to increase the ranking of the previous product.

Sales Rank is relative

Amazon Sales Rank is relative to other products in the market. Thus, the rank is based on the performance of a given product relative to the performance of other products within the same category. For example, if you sell a product and no other seller within the same category makes a sale, your product's Sales Rank goes significantly down compared to the other seller. However, if you sell one product while the other seller sales three products, your rank goes lower but that of the other seller goes significantly lower than yours. The end result is that your Sales Rank goes down in the second scenario but not as low it would if the other seller hadn't made a sale as in the first scenario.

Sales Rank is frequency-sensitive

How frequent you make sales has an impact on your Sales Rank. Products that sell more frequently than others within a given category have lower ranking than those that sell less frequently with the same category. Thus, it is not just about the sales volume but also how many times consumers are looking for your product. This is simply because, Ranking is done on hourly basis and the significance of historical sales is less important compared to the significance of the current sales (of course, time lag of 1 to 3 hours being considered).

For example, if you last sold 15 items 10 days ago and the other seller has been making an average sale of 1 item for the last 10 days, the other seller is more likely to rank higher at the moment though your volume of sales in the last 10 days indicates 15 items while for the other seller it is 10 items.

Sales Rank incorporates performance stability factor

While historical data is given lesser significance over the current data, nonetheless, it is significant in smoothening out fluctuations, especially for seasonal items. For example, if you have been making an average sale of 150 items per day for the last 6 months while the other seller made an average sales of 230 items per day in the first month, 120 in the second month, 50 in the third month 90 in the fourth month, 150 in the fifth month and 220 in the sixth month, it is more likely that you will rank higher. This is because your product has higher performance stability.

Sales Rank is sensitive to customer experience

Sensitivity of the Sales Rank to customer experience is a factor in Amazon's ranking algorithm, though, its impact is not easy to determine unlike the other mentioned factors. Nonetheless, this impact, though significant, is often considered as minor compared to the other mentioned factors.

Customer experience can be indicated by the following;

- Number of positive reviews – the higher the number of positive reviews, the greater the customer experience.
- Number and frequency of customer returns – customers return products for various reasons. However, the most common reason is customer dissatisfaction with the

product quality (defects, late delivery, etc). This indicates poor customer experience with the product.

- Frequency of stock-outs – stock-outs means that customers, especially frequent buyers, miss on utility of the product due to its lack of availability. This definitely brings a negative experience of a continued consumption of the product.

How to use Sales Rank in determining your product performance

Whenever a product is ranked, Amazon presents sponsored ads next to it. This usually comes in the form of "… other (similar) products". This gives you an opportunity to review sponsored ads as an indicator of not only knowing how your product is performing but also what you need to do to improve your sales. To achieve this, check the ranking of those items. Most of the time, those sponsored ads placed next to your product are of lower rank compared to your own. Click on the add to check on the product that not only has lower rank but has more positive reviews and higher volumes of sales. Examine and explore that which makes it achieve these. If need be, you can buy it and sample it out. This will help you know its unique features that make it perform better. You can improve your product based on your findings.

How to use Sales Rank to determine what to sell

Sales Rank is a quick way to determine a product that is performing well in the market. However this is not absolute. You need to take product reviews in conjunction with Sales Rank as parameters for determining what to sell. A product that has a lower Sales Rank accompanied by higher volume of positive reviews plus more volume of sales is a product you need to use as a benchmark in determining what to sell. But, before you fall for the product, establish its profitability. Is it profitable to sell it? If it is profitable to sell it, then, you could as well as have landed on the right product to sell.

HOW TO PRICE YOUR PRODUCTS

Pricing your product is the most important decision you have to make in the market. It determines who should buy your product, by how much and in what quantity. It affects your volumes and profitability. Thus, it is important to have a prudent pricing strategy.

In order to achieve appropriate pricing, you need to know the cost of selling on Amazon;

- your own costs
- Amazon costs

Your own costs;

- Cost of production/purchase – if you are producing the product yourself, you have to incorporate cost of production. However, if you are buying the product for resale, you have to incorporate the cost of purchase (including cost of shipping if incurred by you).
- Cost of shipping to Amazon – whether you produce or purchase for resale, you will need to ship your products to Amazon store/pick-up point. You need to factor this cost.
- Cost of returns – returns are unpredictable. However, if you are dealing with standard products, then, you can estimate the number of likely returns based on experience of those who are already selling your kind of product.

Nonetheless, for a start, you can estimate a certain percentage (e.g. 10%) of provision and keep on adjusting the rate as you gain actual experience of these returns.

Amazon costs;

- Warehouse costs – Amazon charges storage cost for items that have overstayed their duration.
- Membership subscription costs – this cost depends on membership plan. For Individual Seller plan; this is $0.99 per item while for Professional Seller plan; this is $39.99 per month.
- Variable closing costs – This applies only to certain categories of items. Mostly, Videos, Music, Books, Software, Consoles, CDs and DVDs. This rate varies depending on product category, type of shipping service and shipping destination.
- Referral costs – this varies per product category. However it ranges between 6% and 20% for most products. On average, it falls at 15%. There is also minimum referral fee of between $0 and $2.

Determine your profit margin

The following are based for determining your profit margin;

- Based on ROI – Return on Investment (ROI) is what you expect to be compensation for your investment in the product and the entire selling process. For example, you can decide that you deserve 20% ROI. This will a factor on top of the product's total cost (own cost + Amazon cost)

- Based on Opportunity cost – if you are spending $10 to sell an item, how much would you earn if you had invested this $10 in other alternatives? For example, to sell an item on Amazon, you earn $4 profit. If you invested in IPO, you would probably earn $3 and in a mutual fund, $1. Let say this is within a period required to sell one item. Then, the opportunity cost of selling your item on Amazon is $3 (the sacrificed benefit of the next best alternative). Since $4 is higher than $3, your benefit is higher than the opportunity cost. Nonetheless, the price should not be lower than $13 (that is, cost of total cost + opportunity cost).

- Based on market condition – The greatest challenge with near-perfect markets (where there are so many buyers and sellers such that no single buyer or seller can directly influence the market price) such as Amazon, you cannot command a price. Your price has to be in consideration of competitor prices. For example, if your desired minim price is $13 and competitors are selling at $12, then, unless you are also making sales, you need to consider pricing your product at $12 (more so, if you are a new entrant). On the other hand, if your desired minim price is $13 yet competitors are selling at $17, then you need to adjust your price upwards depending on your target volume of sales. If you just have few items, you can sell at $17. However, if you do continuous supply of huge volumes of such item while there is also potentially huge demand for the same in the market, you can opt to price at about $15 so that you can reap big on economies of scale (large scale operations). With economies of scale, there is higher chance that if your costs were $10 per items, you are likely going to negotiate for lower cost or find ways of cutting down costs (especially if you are a producer). This way, you still maintain premium profit margins at a lower price.

Determine the price based on cost + profit margin

Once you have determined your cost and profit margin, you can easily determine your price (= cost + profit margin).

Consider the market dynamics and adjust your price accordingly

The following are market dynamics to factor;

- consumer demand

- seasonal fluctuations
- competitors

Consider pricing strategy that is more appropriate for your product

On the overall, your pricing strategy will determine how you respond to the market in terms of pricing.

The following are major pricing strategies that you can make depending on the market condition;

Penetration pricing – Penetration pricing is a pricing strategy aimed at gaining a greater share of the market by offering lower price than the competition so that you attract more consumers your way. This is great if your product has the capability of capturing and retaining consumer loyalty so that you can reap more from them in future. It is more applicable if there are few players in the market and you have sufficient working capital to patiently wait as the market share picks up. Otherwise, if you have not sufficient working capital muscle, you may get worn out and exit the market just when the market share had started optimizing.

Premium pricing – Premium pricing is more appropriate when you are introducing a new and very unique product into the market. In this case, you price your product at a rate much higher than the competition to reward yourself for creating a superior quality product (and in essence, punish your competition for presenting inferior product in the market). This is a great strategy when you know that it will take long for any competitor to be able to discover your unique formula and thus compete with you (more so, if your product is patented). It also works well when you know that consumers in that segment are much eager for products of higher value and are only forced to do with that which is currently available in the market.

Economy pricing – This is a pricing strategy that is pursued when the economies of scale are in one's favor. Only a small margin of profit is charged, but, since the goods are produced and sold in large scale, the overall revenue and profits hit the required target. Though, without economies of scale, it is simply the equilibrium price you would expect in the market.

Skimming price – This is a price that takes advantage of market willing to give a higher value for your product. Thus, you skim what consumers are willing to give over and above what ought to be the equilibrium price. You continue doing this as you adjust the price downwards as what the consumers are willing to give recedes until the equilibrium price is attained. Skimming price is more appropriate when there is higher demand for your product than normal. You raise the price to avoid unintended stock-out and keep adjusting until such a point where the demand for your product and the supply of it reaches equilibrium.

Psychological pricing – Psychological pricing refers to a host of strategies that are pegged on consumer psychology. For example, an item priced at $9.99 is more likely to appear cheaper to the buyer than an item priced at $10. Other types of psychological pricing strategies include;

- **Repulsive similarity** – If two products are priced the same, consumers are more likely to suspend their buy decision. This is because neither of them offers a decision-edge over the other. Thus, make sure that your pricing is unique.

- **Price anchoring** – When two products of similar nature; one with a price tag of $1500 and another with a price tag of $7500 are positioned together in the same space, the one of $1500 looks like a super-bargain. Yet, when the one of $1500 is positioned near a one of $50, then the one of $1500 looks a premium product. Thus, by placing premium products near standard products you can create a sense of premium value in the mind of potential customers who will consider the less expensive item as a super-bargain. This is a great pricing strategy if you are dealing with items targeting customers who value prestige such as jewelry, cars, high-end houses, etc.

- **Time-vs-Saving** - When it comes to leisure, recreational or items which consumers are more inclined towards its time utility as opposed to financial savings, then, emphasizing on how long the benefit lasts as opposed to how much saving can be made is the best choice. This too can apply to products like cosmetics, dyes, etc.

- **Was-Now reduction** – Though pretty traditional, without it being overused, showing how big a product's price has gone down (e.g. Was $80, Now $59) can create an impression super-bargain and big savings on the buyers psychology. Adding the urgency "new prices valid while stock last" can help to hasten buy decision. This strategy is ideal if you are dealing with customers who like super-bargains.

- **Minimize the number of price digits as possible** – when an item is priced at $9,999.00, it appears more expensive compared to a similar item priced at $9,999. Yet still, an item priced at $9,999 appears more expensive than a similar item priced at $9999. The lesser the number of digits the lesser the quantity is impressed in the memory. Higher memory consumption can create a mistaken impression of a gigantic price which is likely to dissuade a customer from making a buy decision.

What is important to note is that psychological factors don't cut across board. Thus, it is important to study consumer behavior within your respective market segment to understand their psychology. This will enable you to implement the most appropriate psychological pricing strategy.

CONCLUSION

Thank you for having committed yourself to acquiring and reading this book.

The world of ecommerce is transforming the way business is done. It provides opportunities for both full-time sellers and part-time sellers to earn some income. Amazon is a world leader in ecommerce in as far as buying and selling of consumer products is concern. Whether you intend to start-off full-time or part-time, Amazon is a great place for you.

To build your online business requires a solid foundation. You need a blueprint. This guide, "Blueprint to Selling on Amazon" is your great companion in this endeavor. It provides proven practical hands-on information in a beginner-approach that responds to all your likely needs. With this guide, you can easily start selling on Amazon and make at least $2000 a month profit on side income, part time. With automation, however little time you have, it is sufficient to enable you create multiple passive income streams on Amazon. Amazon itself recognizes this. That is why it has created Amazon Seller App, a mobile App that can help you sell on Amazon while on the go.

It is my sincere hope that this guide has not only provided relevant information about selling on Amazon but has also inspired you to start off and become a successful Seller making $2000 or more a month profit on side income, part time.

Again, thank you for acquiring and reading this book.

www.ingramcontent.com/pod-product-compliance
Lightning Source LLC
Chambersburg PA
CBHW071516210326
41597CB00018B/2776